1

The First People used fish for food.

How did they catch the fish?

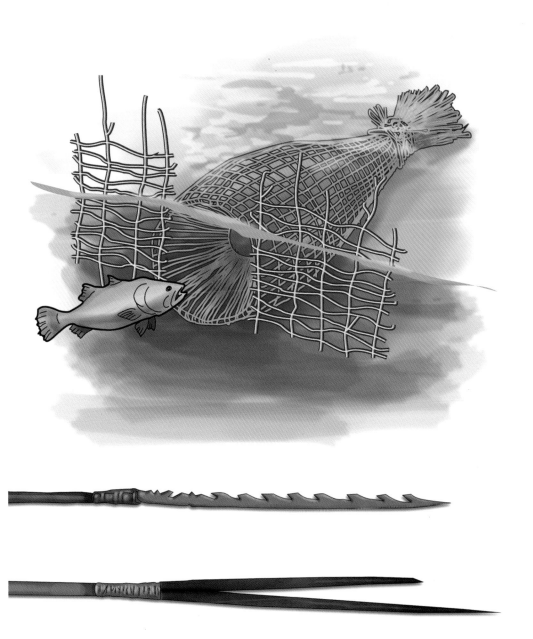

Rock traps were used in the sea.

At low tide the fish were caught with nets.

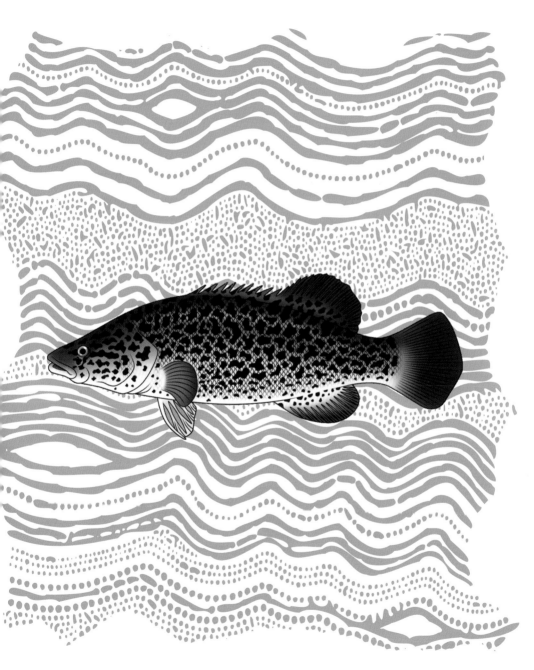

Fish could be speared from a canoe.

11

Eels were caught in traps.

Fish were caught with a hook.

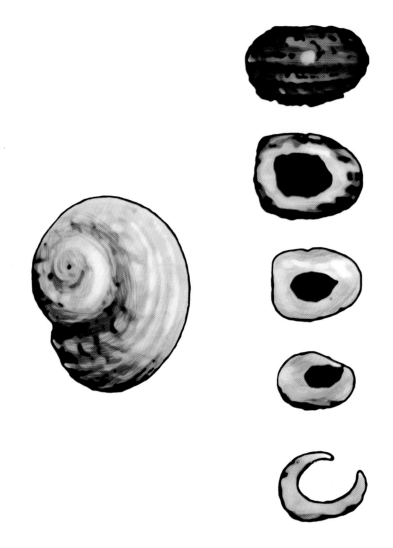

Baskets were used in rivers to catch fish.

17

Fish could be caught with nets.

Dugongs were eaten as food.

20

A whale was found on the sand.

Word bank

fish   catch

catch   dugongs

rock   eaten

traps   whale

caught

tide

speared

canoe

eels

hook

baskets

rivers